Living Unscripted

Life is Improv. Learn the Rules.
Be Successful.

By Ben Winter
Contributions by Tara Hedberg

Living Unscripted

Life is Improv. Learn the Rules.
Be Successful.

ISBN-13: 978-0-9992944-6-8

Copyright © 2017 by Ben Winter. All Rights Reserved.

Special thanks to:

Patricia Winter
Mandell Winter Jr.
PSI Seminars
Madcap Theater, Westminster, CO
Rodents of Unusual Size Improv Comedy Troupe

1

Where's Your Script?

Wake up!!!

Quick, read your script!

You know, the one for the entire day. Quick!!!

You have five minutes to read it and memorize it because you have a day to get to!

Hurry!!!

Oh, and not only do you need to memorize your schedule, but all of the unanticipated changes, shifts and problems that will arise; every conversational dialogue needs to be memorized, every second planned!

And remember – no deviations allowed! Stick to the plan. The clock's ticking! GO! GO! GO!

Imagine waking up every morning with the daunting task of memorizing a script for your day. Picture it: Memorizing every conversation, every spontaneous decision, every unexpected encounter... Exhausting, right? In reality, this task would be not just tedious but downright impossible. Even the most talented actors occasionally slip a word or ad-lib a line. The fact is, life doesn't give us a script.

Instead, our lives resemble a continuous, unscripted improv show. We create, adapt, and react in real-time, every second of every day. Yet, many of us may not recognize this spontaneous performance art in our daily routines or understand its simple yet transformative rules.

Consider the beloved TV show, "Whose Line Is It Anyway?" Its charm and success rest on a foundational principle: all participants adhere to a shared set of improv rules. A local improv show that leaves you cringing might have a performer breaking these rules, creating discord with the group. But a show that leaves you spellbound? That's pure improv magic, with all performers in sync.

Let's demystify what we mean by 'improv' here. Beyond the standup comedy realm, improv is about a collective journey, with participants weaving stories without predetermined routes or narratives.

Improv...

> *"The art or act of improvising, or of composing, uttering, executing, or arranging anything without previous preparation."*

— Dictionary.com

Isn't that an apt description of life itself? We don't know whom we'll bump into at the grocery store or what unexpected event might disrupt our meticulously planned meeting. It's like being plucked from the audience, thrust onto the stage, and simply told to "GO!" For many, it's a nightmarish scenario akin to public speaking—oft cited as one of humanity's greatest fears. But this is what life demands from us every single moment.

However, the secret sauce to navigating this constant improvisation isn't merely about surviving; it's about thriving. We've evolved not just to cope with the unpredictability but to embrace and master it. With the right mindset and tools, we can turn life's unscripted moments into masterful performances. Ready to take the stage?

What if there was a better way?

An easier way?

2
The Game

Ever heard the phrase, "Life's a game"? It's not just a catchy saying; it encapsulates a deeper truth. Every game, from the simplest board game to the most complex sports, operates on a set of rules. By understanding and adhering to these rules, we find clarity, strategy, and enjoyment.

Consider the elegance of chess. In this game, each piece has its specific move, its role, its purpose. If players whimsically moved pieces without regard to these rules, the game would descend into chaos. Strategies would crumble, victories would lose meaning, and the very essence of the game would be lost. Instead, when both players respect the rules, chess becomes a dance of intellect and anticipation.

Hockey is no different. Picture a rink where every player abides by their own personal rulebook. Referees would be rendered powerless, and the beautiful choreography of team play would dissolve into a disorganized free-for-all. Yet, when everyone is on the same page, the game becomes an exhilarating display of skill, strategy, and teamwork.

Children, with their boundless imagination, often craft games on-the-fly. It's amusing, and sometimes exasperating, to see them modify rules as they go. Take the seemingly straightforward foam dart gun battle. One moment, a single hit spells 'game over', but when the tables turn, suddenly it's 'three hits to win'. This ever-shifting rulebook can frustrate adults who crave a consistent framework.

At its core, this quest for rules stems from a desire for clear expectations. Life, in all its unpredictability, is much like these games. And just like improv, which many view with trepidation due to its spontaneous nature, life also thrives on certain unspoken rules.

Why do so many remain oblivious to these rules? Simply put, most have never been taught them, making it impossible to pass them on. Today's fast-paced world, characterized by dwindling attention spans, craves instant gratification. In the realm of improv, this translates to wanting that immediate laughter. But much like life, the best moments in improv aren't always instantaneous; they build and crescendo.

The beauty is, when you're equipped with life's playbook, everything changes. Challenges become opportunities. Insults turn into moments of humor. You can stand firm amidst chaos, laughing in the face of adversity and seeing the lighter side of life.

Wouldn't it be empowering to have a compass that guides you confidently in any situation? To view obstacles not as setbacks, but as part of the game's strategy? With the right understanding, life can be not just a game, but a thrilling adventure filled with laughter, growth, and endless possibilities.

It can happen.

And this is how it happened...

3

How This Book and my Company, Success Improv, LLC, Came to Be

The cocoon of adolescence and my early twenties was woven with threads of self-doubt. While most harbored dreams of love and relationships, my shaky self-confidence held me back. College days slipped by, and while many found partners, I was left searching. Then, serendipity intervened in the form of a personal growth seminar. Their promise? A better relationship. With hope in my heart, I delved deep into years of learning, yet, despite acquiring knowledge, implementation remained a challenge.

In time, the universe had its way. I met someone, dated, and finally had that relationship I always wanted. However, a lurking discontent persisted. Until improv came knocking.

Following my girlfriend's lead, I entered the world of improv, a domain I'd always viewed from the outside, too insecure to step in. But oh, what an exhilarating discovery it was! With the structured rules of improv, the weight of expectations lifted. Who'd have thought that rules could be so liberating?

Six weeks of beginner improv, multiple classes, numerous performances, and the bug had bit me. I thirsted for more. Yet, life always has its curveballs. An invitation to audition for an improv troupe led to an unexpected redirection to another troupe. Once more, apprehension and unfamiliarity shadowed me. Luckily, I had improv and personal growth to push me through.

A decade later, armed with personal growth insights, life experiences ranging from quitting a long-term job, to navigating a divorce, and an unwavering passion for improv, I hit a personal rock bottom. But from the depths emerged a vision, radiant and potent – the inception of 'Success Improv'.

However, every vision requires realization. And for that, I needed more than just self-belief. I needed a partner in crime, someone with shared experiences, mutual trust, and unwavering passion. Tara Hedberg was that missing puzzle piece. Our shared journey in personal growth and years of performing improv together had laid a foundation of trust. Together, with her insights complementing mine, Success Improv was destined to flourish.

After rigorous testing, tweaking, and the invaluable input of business coaches, Success Improv was ready for the world. What you are reading now is the culmination of decades of personal and collective evolution.

Join us, as we share the treasure trove of insights and tools we've refined over years, ensuring your journey is just as transformative. Dive into our world, where improvisation isn't just an art – it's a way of life.

What are the rules of life?

What are the rules of improv?

4

The Rules of Improv

Imagine you're on the cusp of constructing an architectural marvel—a skyscraper that will define skylines. Before you dream of its magnificence, you first think of its foundation. That's where the magic begins. Similarly, in the grand design of life, the rules of improv act as the bedrock and foundation upon which you anchor all your endeavors.

A robust foundation isn't just about bearing weight; it's about resilience. It empowers you to weather life's metaphorical earthquakes, stand tall against its tsunamis, and emerge unscathed from its hurricanes. When your foundation is solid, not only do you become an unyielding force, but you also unlock a world of endless possibilities.

You might wonder: with a myriad of rules that improv offers, where does one begin? The beauty is, while the vast realm of improv provides a rich tapestry of guidelines, mastering a select few can set you on a transformative journey. Let's delve into the **top five quintessential rules** of improv. These aren't just theatrical tips; they are life principles, ready to enhance everything from your personal relationships to your professional endeavors, encompassing spheres like health, spirituality, finances, and beyond.

Embrace these foundational tenets, and witness how a mere performance art can translate into a masterclass for life!

The five main rules of improv are:

Don't Deny

Yes, And…

Be Specific

Focus on the Present

Trust

On the surface, it all appears straightforward, doesn't it? Yet, as with many things in life, there's a depth beneath that surface simplicity. Most are unaware of the profound implications these rules carry, not just in the realm of improv, but in the intricate dance of life itself.

Merely skimming the surface of these rules, many fall into the trap of subjective interpretation, tweaking them based on personal perceptions. But isn't that a bit like playing a game without fully understanding its rules? This way, the essence gets altered, potentially leading us astray.

Therefore, a mere introduction won't suffice. To truly harness their power, these rules demand clarity and comprehensive understanding. By delineating each rule's parameters, we aren't just setting boundaries; we're establishing a clear roadmap. This ensures that each rule complements the others, creating a harmonious symphony where no single note overshadows the others.

So, let's not just skim the surface. Dive deep, decode the essence, and discover the transformative potential of each rule in both improv and the grand theater of life!

Let us begin with

rule number 1...

5

Rule #1

"Don't Deny"

The first rule of improv – Don't Deny

If you were to approach a seasoned improv artist and ask about the cardinal rule, their response would invariably echo one sentiment: **"Don't Deny."** They might label it differently - "Say yes", "Agree with" or even **"Yes, And…"**. The latter is often touted as the primary rule of improv, but it has layers of its own, a story for, well, the next chapter. The essence of **"Don't Deny?"** It's all about embracing reality: "Accepting What Is".

So, what does this mean in the world of improv? It's about receiving with open arms - be it inputs from co-performers, cues from the audience, or constraints of the scenario. It translates to an acknowledgment: "This is my reality, right here, right now. No denials."

Consider a scene: Two male actors emerge. The first declares, "Mom, I broke my arm today." The audience sees two men, but instantly, the second actor has been handed the 'mother' role. By embracing this unexpected twist, the actors can weave a scene dripping with brilliance. But a refusal? It's akin to throwing a wrench in the machine. The audience is left adrift, actors falter, and the scene crumbles. The aftermath? An ambiguous narrative, reminiscent of a chaotic children's game where rules morph on a whim. Embrace the given, however, and you might just craft a scene that leaves the audience spellbound.

Beyond the stage, life unfurls with a script brimming with twists. Broken cars, lost love, financial hiccups, heartbreaks – challenges abound. And yes, there are delightful chapters too, but those are easily embraced. The real hurdle? Facing adversity head-on.

Many remain ensnared by the past, imprisoned by denial. The truth? What occurred, occurred. Embracing this reality unlocks a healing power. It's a sentiment most therapists would vouch for. Acceptance isn't a mere concept; it's a catalyst for progress.

This acceptance births tranquility. It unfurls a realm of endless potential rather than barricades.

But how does one embrace the unpleasant? The road to acceptance, while straightforward, demands immense strength. It's about granting ourselves a mere three seconds, a brief pause to recognize the truth of the moment. Our innate instinct is to react impulsively, but by pressing that metaphorical pause button, we gift ourselves clarity and awareness.

So, when life's curveballs hit, take that moment.

Take three seconds.

Laugh in the face of adversity, introspect about the journey, or simply hold back that impulsive reaction. The key? Just stop, breathe, acknowledge, and then? Dive right into rule number two to navigate the challenge.

In improv, as in life, acceptance is the opening act. Allowing you to respond, not just react. And remember, with every acceptance, you're setting the stage for a performance - or a life - that resonates, touches, and inspires.

And how do you respond?

6

Rule #2

"Yes, And.."

The second rule of improv – "Yes, And…"

Often hailed as the primal commandment of improv by many, **"Yes, And…"** is not just two words. It's a philosophy, a method, an approach. But why do we introduce it as the second rule in this discussion? It's simple. The **"Yes"** is our handshake with the first rule: an affirmation, a nod to acceptance. The beauty lies in the **"And"**, a subtle yet powerful word that propels things forward, keeping the momentum alive.

But vs. And: The Game-Changer

Consider these two conjunctions: "But" and "And". The former, though seemingly harmless, has the ability to nullify everything before it. It's the equivalent of saying, "I value your perspective, **but**...". The undertone? Dismissal. Contrastingly, "And" amplifies, builds, and acknowledges. Think of "I understand your view, "**and**" I have another perspective." This word expands possibilities, making conversations inclusive.

Let's delve into an illustration:

"I love you, "**but**" you drive me crazy with your TV binges."

versus

"I love you, "**and**" you drive me crazy with your TV binges."

The distinction? The former questions love itself, while the latter accepts love and merely addresses a concern.

On the Improv Stage

Recall the "Mom, I broke my arm" scene. A "Yes, but" response can rupture the flow, undermining the narrative set by the first actor.

If the response is, "Oh, your arm is broken? But it isn't." Now nobody believes it is broken and it negates what the first actor did to establish the scene. The actor accepted being the mom (in this instance) but didn't add to the scene. Instead, the actor took something away.

What if they added to the scene? What are the possibilities?

They could have said, "Oh honey, at least you got a bright red cast. Red is your favorite color." In that instance they **added** that it had already been fixed. And that the child likes the color red. It also implies that someone else took the kid to the hospital to get it fixed. By doing a **"Yes, And…"** the actor added to the scene to help it progress.

Another approach could be to act as though this child's broken arm is the worst thing that ever happened and start freaking out, "Oh No! We have to get to the hospital quick! This can't be happening! Not my child! Does it hurt? Do you want a bandage? What do we do? Does your dad know? How did this happen?" and so on. This approach would add to the scene subjectively by showing how crazy the mom is and how she handles a situation. Again, this moves the scene forward. The actors can add to what has been added. And they must accept the new information as "what is". They must not deny the new information.

Starting to see how these rules continually interact with one another?

The scene's magic is truly unleashed with **"Yes, And…"**, like acknowledging the broken arm and adding, information about the cast.

Whether it's portraying an over-anxious mother or adding new dimensions to the scene, the **"Yes, And…"** philosophy fuels progress and stimulates creativity. In essence, it synergizes with our first rule, perpetually intertwining to weave captivating stories.

Beyond the Stage:
The Power of "Yes, And…" in Life

Brainstorming sessions are a quintessential example. Imagine a family planning a reunion. A collaborative environment where every idea is built upon, rather than shut down, not only strengthens bonds but might just birth the most legendary reunion plan!

If everyone who offers an idea is shot down by someone else in the room, how likely are they to share any more ideas that come up. The brainstorming comes to an end rather quickly, there is resentment in the room, and a lack of trust and understanding for each other.

How often in life do we not speak up or share ideas because we are afraid of them being shot down? How much does this stop us?

Given enough time, and enough **"Yes, and's"** that family could come up with some of the best ideas any family has ever had for a family reunion. This becomes a much more fun exercise with much better results.

In the business sphere, this principle is monumental. Company A's potential game-changing product can only truly be realized when everyone's voice is valued. Every idea, regardless of its immediate utility, contributes. It's the collective **"Yes, And…"** approach that fosters innovation, creativity, and breakthroughs. If everyone's ideas are shot down, nobody would ever get to the game-changing idea that sets the world in motion.

Nobody wants to be wrong.

If you make them wrong by denying all of their ideas, they shut down or fight back.

Similarly, when brainstorming individually, it's essential to be your best supporter. Discarding your ideas is like denying potential innovations. It's crucial to cultivate an environment of acceptance and progress, whether in your mind or in a meeting room.

To sum it up, **"Yes, And…"** isn't just a rule for improv. It's a transformative mantra that, when applied, can enrich narratives, deepen relationships, and pave the way for unparalleled creativity. In improv and life, the beauty lies in embracing what is and then paving the way for what can be.

Speaking of making people or yourself wrong...

7

"Yes, And..." Part 2

Have you ever been trapped in an argument, desperately trying to prove a point, only to find the more you resist, the stronger the opposition grows? Enter the **"Yes, And"** principle, a nuanced tactic not just for improv, but for everyday communication too.

Being Right vs. Being Effective

No one particularly relishes the idea of being wrong. And being "told" you're wrong? That's even worse. It triggers our defenses, sending us into a battle mode where every word becomes a weapon. Politics, family dinners, corporate meetings – it's a scene we've all witnessed. The beauty of **"Yes, And"** is that it allows individuals to gently steer conversations, presenting information in a manner that leads people to self-realization.

Transforming Scenes: Improv's Magic

For example, in improv, suppose a pair of players are on stage and are playing a scene that is just not going anywhere. Another player has the chance to enter the scene and make it more exciting. To do this in a way that supports the scene and the original players, the new player does not fight with what has already been started.

A scene that was established with two people cooking, very politely and calmly, can be energized by a third player running on and saying "Guys, I know you want these meals to be perfect, and I am so glad you are committed to greatness, but the customers are about to riot if I don't bring them some food NOW!" All of a sudden, the perfectionist chefs have an exciting scene to play with, the conflict comes between perfectionism and timeliness, which could be fun for the audience because they recognize that struggle.

In contrast the third player could run into the scene yelling at the players to get the led out because people are starving, and while it may get a quick laugh, the other players will be embarrassed and frustrated, and the group dynamic will be damaged. Then, instead of playing with a fact of modern life, it becomes a fight between the primary players and the interloper, which is usually very unentertaining. There are plenty of outlets to see people scream at each other and it is simply not funny or entertaining. Screaming isn't the only way to invigorate a scene.

The Real-World Applications

Outside of improv, consider work scenarios. Suppose a colleague criticizes your approach. The knee-jerk reaction might be to retaliate. But what if you respond with, "Ordinarily, I'd share your perspective, "and" I've received additional insights that suggest this approach will work better." Instantly, the conversation shifts from adversarial to collaborative.

Or consider educators. A frustrated parent confronts a teacher, claiming their child is an 'angel' at home. Instead of getting defensive, the teacher might say, "I'm sure he's wonderful at home, "and" we notice a change in his behavior around his peers, here at school. How can we ensure consistency?" Such a response not only validates the parent's perspective but also shifts the focus to a collaborative solution. By not making the parents wrong about their beliefs of their child, they added new information to help the parents think about the situation differently.

The Underlying Philosophy: Understanding & Collaboration

At its core, **"Yes, And"** champions understanding. It gently nudges conversations from confrontational stand-offs to collaborative discussions. Whether on stage or in the boardroom, it's a tool that fosters harmony, promotes growth, and often leads to the most innovative solutions.

After all, isn't a world with more understanding, patience, and cooperation something we all yearn for?

When you *"Yes, and"* you must ...

Wait for it...

Getting closer...

Maybe take a break?

Nah...

Proceed to the next page now?

8

Rule #3

Be Specific

"Be specific!" It might sound like simple advice, but its implications are profound, especially in the captivating world of improv. To truly grasp its essence, let's unravel this with vivid examples and everyday scenarios.

Crafting the Scene: Specificity in Improv

Imagine two actors taking center stage. One exclaims, "I spilled it!" Instant confusion envelops the atmosphere. The co-actor is left stranded, grappling for clues. What was spilled? Why is it crucial? The identity of their characters remains an enigma. The audience, equally baffled, is left dangling on the edge of curiosity. Such ambiguity doesn't lay a fertile ground for creativity; it stifles it.

Now, let's switch gears. Instead, the actor articulates, "Honey, I spilled paint on our brand-new carpet while redecorating the living room." A vivid narrative instantly unfolds. The scene is ripe with potential, and both the actors and the audience are thrust into a colorful world of possibilities. The drama can now unfold organically, thanks to that specific spark.

Real-life Resonance: The Subtleties of Specificity

Take the common domestic request: "Honey, please take out the trash." Sounds straightforward, doesn't it? However, buried beneath this plea lies a maze of unspoken expectations.

Let's create an even more detailed picture: The husband, engrossed in a football match, hears the request. Hours whizz by, the second game begins and concludes, but the trash remains untouched. The wife's bubbling frustration finally erupts into fiery rage. A trivial chore has now snowballed into a domestic dispute.

But what if the wife had opted for specificity? "Honey, could you take out the trash **now**? It's emitting an unpleasant odor." By elucidating the 'what,' 'when,' and 'why,' she eliminates ambiguity. With clear expectations set, the husband is in a position to align his actions or negotiate based on his preferences.

Unearthing the Core: The Power of Clear Expectations

At its heart, the principle of specificity isn't just about clarity; it's fundamentally about managing and communicating expectations. Whether you're captivating an audience in an improv act or navigating the intricate dance of daily life, ***"being specific"*** paves the path for understanding and harmony. Remember, it's not just about what you want to convey; it's about ensuring the message is received as intended. Specificity, in essence, is the bridge that connects intent with understanding.

A profound revelation awaits us, cloaked in the fabric of everyday emotions. Let's unravel it by journeying back to our earlier example.

Consider the wife, exasperated with the trash still sitting around. Underlying her frustration is an unmet expectation. This brings us to a pivotal observation:

> "The only reason anyone ever gets upset is because an expectation hasn't been met."

By recognizing this pattern, one can introspect: "Why am I feeling this way? What expectation wasn't satisfied?" Many times, we're blind to our own anticipations until they're dashed, and emotions flare up. Recognizing this is paramount.

Remember rule number one: **"Don't Deny."** Don't dismiss your previously unrecognized expectations. Avoid the trap of denial. Accept that you might've held an implicit expectation and, crucially, never communicated it. Until voiced, how can others cater to it or even negotiate it?

With this acknowledgment, we transition to rule number two: **"Yes, And."** It's an opportunity to share and reshape the narrative, bringing clarity to previously murky waters. For instance, the wife could have rephrased, "Honey, I hoped you'd take out the trash immediately because it's foul-smelling. Could you do it now?" Isn't this more constructive than venting frustration?

Ensuring clarity upfront by setting clear expectations is ideal. However, if emotions do rise, pausing, reflecting, and pinpointing the missed expectation offers a route to harmony. Think of it as a dance between preempting conflicts and rectifying them.

Consider these instances:

- Upset because you're unwell?

Expectation: You assumed you'd always be in good health.

- Grieving a loved one?

Expectation: You believed they'd be around longer or wished to express certain feelings before their departure.

- Disheartened by a missed job opportunity?

Expectation: You anticipated being the chosen candidate.

- Annoyed the store ran out of your favorite product?

Expectation: You expected it to be readily available.

- Frustrated with traffic snarls and wondering about the competence of other drivers? Well, maybe your expectations of perfect traffic are a tad optimistic. (Yes, I grapple with this daily too!)

In essence, whenever we're perturbed, the flip side often reveals a preset expectation. While sometimes you can renegotiate reality with others, at other times, it's about reconciling with the situation. The power of **"Yes, And"** then transforms into making the best out of what's beyond our control.

This seamlessly bridges us to rule number three: **"Be Specific."** After identifying your feelings and unearthing the root expectation, it's pivotal to express it clearly. This triad of rules isn't isolated but rather a continuous loop, guiding our emotions and interactions.

With diligence and practice, one can fluidly maneuver through these rules, harmonizing expectations and emotions in mere moments. Remember, understanding the heartbeats of your emotions means understanding your expectations. And that, dear reader, is a powerful tool for life!

The best point to start practicing is when you notice you are upset.

> Being upset is the most recognizable point that one or more of these rules aren't being followed.

To notice you are upset you must…

Here it comes…

You're not ready for this. Are you?

Sure you are!

Go for it!

Turn the page!

9

Rule #4
Focus on the Present

Immerse yourself in the heart of improv, and a principle emerges, shimmering with utmost importance: Rule four - **"Focus on the Present."** This isn't just a call to be aware, but a clarion call to truly live in the heartbeat of the moment.

Imagine a scene on stage. If your mind is a wandering caravan, contemplating chores, deadlines, or that frustrating conversation at work, you're bound to miss the essence of the act. Doing so in improv is as detrimental as uttering a "yes, but". It's counterproductive. It's like attempting to row a boat with no oars. The beauty of **"Yes, And"** can only bloom if you're truly present.

Visualize this: Let's say actor one says, "...and then we went to into the cave and the lights stopped working." The actor who wasn't paying attention could end up saying, "Yeah, cooking in the dark sucks. Especially since our kitchen isn't laid out like normal kitchens." Chaos ensues. The story thread frays. Sure, advanced improv artists might salvage the scene, but for many, it's a scene going downhill. Being present could prevent such a derailing.

World-class negotiators are maestros of the present. They don't just listen; they absorb—catching spoken words and the silent cues alike. They artfully steer conversations, leading the counterpart to forge solutions that resonate with everyone. This "buy-in" from both parties makes the agreement steadfast.

Think of car salespeople. They epitomize this rule. They attune to you, crafting a narrative wherein buying that car becomes your idea. They masterfully lead you there by capitalizing on each word you say, every hesitation you display. The power of now, right?

Of course, these skills can be exploited. But it's essential to highlight that the spirit of **"Focus on the Present"** isn't to manipulate. Choose to misuse it, and, well, that's your karma.

Embracing the present bestows a sense of liberation. Worries about the future or about past regrets dissipate. It's like reliving those carefree days of childhood where the world was just your playground, and every moment was the whole universe.

Ever been on a date, only to find your companion buried in their phone? That digital distraction is a breach of this rule. It screams, "I'm elsewhere!" How can genuine connections form if one isn't genuinely present? And how often have we heard or uttered the piercing question in relationships: "Are you even listening to me?"

At its core, the essence of **"Focus on the Present"** champions fostering genuine relationships and deep understanding. It promotes a thoughtful response over a hasty reaction. Recognizing and applying this rule, you earn not just the trust of others but also fortify trust in yourself.

So, as the world hurtles on, take a pause. Breathe. Immerse in the moment. Because life, just like improv, unfolds in the magic of the now.

In other words, you create, and now have....

10

Rule #5

Trust

Dive into the enigmatic world of improv, and you unearth a foundation built upon a set of principles. But there's a keystone—perhaps more ethereal than tangible—that holds it all together: **"Trust."** It's not a rule etched in stone; it's the subtle alchemy birthed by abiding by the first four rules. A rich tapestry woven through consistency, understanding, and mutual respect.

Consider **"trust"** not just as a rule, but as the golden thread tying everything together. It's not about naively giving it away but harnessing the profound power of intuition—the compass within that rarely, if ever, misleads. While trusting the sketchy stranger in a dimly lit alley is questionable, trusting your instincts about that situation is paramount.

Immerse yourself in the world of performance improv, and you'll find troupes, like intricate dances of camaraderie, perfecting their craft over time. These artists become attuned to each other's rhythms, quirks, and nuances. They keenly understand when rules are stretched or bent, and through this journey, they forge an unbreakable bond of **"trust"**. It's no wonder then that the most spellbinding performances emanate from troupes that **"trust"** profoundly in one another.

Drawing parallels to the grand theater of life, the same holds true. When you and your tribe march to the beat of these universal improv rules, **"trust"** flourishes. The ripple effects are profound—harmonious interactions, deeper connections, and love in abundance.

Now, bring this lens to the corporate arena. **"trust"** is the elixir that fuels success. Reflect on micromanagement, that stifling approach that douses creativity. It's the antithesis of **"trust"**. It's a cacophonous tango where neither party believes in the other. Yet, when **"trust"** is cultivated, the dynamics transform. Employees, when trusted, strive to exceed expectations. Managers, when trusting, cultivate empowered teams that innovate and thrive. It's a symphony where respect is the melody, and success, the inevitable crescendo.

This beautiful domino effect becomes evident: understanding nurtures **"trust"**, trust paves the way for happiness, and happiness inevitably blossoms into love.

Contemplate those in your life to whom you've given the keys to your heart. Those you'd follow into a storm or entrust with your most cherished treasures. Isn't it fascinating that the bedrock of such deep-seated **"trust"** can be traced back to the foundational rules of improv? Even if it wasn't apparent before, a closer look reveals the intricate dance of these principles in play.

In essence, while **"trust"** in improv might be an "unspoken rule," its resonance echoes far and wide, permeating every act, every scene, and every relationship.

But...But...

Yes, everyone has THAT But...

No...not that butt!

This but...

11

What if I am the only...

It's that proverbial elephant in the room. As you stand at the crossroads of mastering the art of improv, you're confronted with a pivotal query: "What if I am the lone ranger on this journey?"

But let's flip the script.

Imagine the one person you engage in conversation with incessantly, day in and day out. Spoiler alert: It's **you**. Ah yes, that silent dialogue, the ceaseless inner banter, and the countless soliloquies. And here's a revelation: Talking to oneself, when laced with love and positivity, isn't just sane—it's therapeutic.

Now, pivot that lens inward. Think of all those lofty self-promises. "I'll crush it at the gym daily." Oops, missed again. "Embarking on a diet odyssey." Detoured by that irresistible cheesecake. "That bestseller I've been dreaming of writing." Well, the TV series took precedence. Recognize the pattern? Those unfulfilled pledges metamorphosing into inner critics. But here's your improvisation toolkit at play. Embrace the "accept what is" mantra. Engage in a **"Yes, And"** dialogue with your inner self. Ground yourself in the present, reshaping your mindset and recalibrating your course.

The magic of improv doesn't merely orbit your interactions with others—it begins with the relationship you cultivate with your inner self. And trust us, trusting yourself is the cornerstone. It's the first step to self-love, the foundation of true well-being.

Yet, what unfolds when you're armed with the improv arsenal, and the world remains oblivious? Navigating this terrain is akin to mastering a dance. A dance where your partner hasn't learned the steps yet. Yet, even when they veer off course, you recalibrate, leading with grace, understanding, and patience. They might be oblivious to the dance, but you lead, guide, and steer with finesse, making the dance appear seamless.

It's a reality we've all grappled with - you can't mold others, only your reactions. In this journey, as you dance to the rhythms of improv, you metamorphose. Your perspective shifts. Frustrations fade as humor takes center stage. You find joy in the chaos, serenity amidst the cacophony. For in your heart, you know the rules of improv. And with them, you turn every stumblingblock into a steppingstone, making each day an enthralling improv performance.

Life, much like a grand board game, is replete with rules. But here's the secret sauce: once you discern the guidelines, the pathways to success and happiness unfold like a well-penned script. You're not just a player; you're the MVP, the strategist, the winner. Armed with the rules, you're not just surviving - you're thriving. Victory? It's already in your pocket.

Take a moment and visualize your next move. With every challenge, see an opportunity; with every stumble, find a lesson. The game board of life is vast, but with the right strategies, every move you make propels you closer to your goals.

So, unshackle those inhibitions, dive headfirst, and seize the day! Prosperity beckons, joy awaits, and success is just around the corner. As you navigate this enthralling journey, may you be enveloped in a profound love - a love for oneself, a cherishing of others, and an unwavering passion for the vibrant tapestry of life.

Now, with the playbook in hand and fervor in your heart, embark on this grand adventure. Play passionately, love deeply, and let the symphony of life play its most enchanting tune for you.

Don't Deny

Yes, And…

Be Specific

Focus on the Present

Trust

Learn how to succeed with classes from

SuccessImprov.com

Learn More about Expectations at

HavingExpectations.com

Understanding Expectations

Leads to Peace

Read More of Ben Winter's Books

Fiction and Non-Fiction

MrImprov.com

The Shadow Puppet Trilogy

"The Wrong Turn"

"The Wrong Choice"

"The Wrong Time"

"The Worst Idea"

"A Sleep Through Time"

www.ingramcontent.com/pod-product-compliance
Lightning Source LLC
Chambersburg PA
CBHW070124100426
42744CB00010B/1914